EVERY BIRD IS ONE BIRD

Signed

Every Bird is One Bird

Francine Sterle

TUPELO PRESS
Dorset, Vermont

Every Bird Is One Bird

ISBN 0-9710310-1-0

Printed in Canada

Library of Congress Control Number: 2001132519

Acknowledgments

Grateful acknowledgment is made to the following, in which these poems first appeared, some in earlier versions.

CRANIA: *Making a Cross* and *Snake*

EKPHRASIS: *Triskelion*

GREAT RIVER REVIEW: *After Visiting a Nature Conservancy Volunteer*

THE HARRISBURG REVIEW: *Fracture* and *Reflection*

THE MIDWEST QUARTERLY: *Habitat*

NIMROD: Sections 6 & 7, *The Hive* and Sections 7-14, *Certain Moments Come*. Full text of *The Hive* subsequently appeared in THE DRUNKEN BOAT.

THE NORTH AMERICAN REVIEW: *Deciphering the Alphabet*

ROSEBUD: *Raven Watch*

SIDEWALKS: *The Octopus*

THE SOW'S EAR POETRY REVIEW: *Two Women*

In addition, *Entering the Landscape* and *Second Sight* were anthologized in 33 MINNESOTA POETS (Nodin Press, 2000), and a few of the poems in this manuscript first appeared in a chapbook entitled *The White Bridge* (Poetry Harbor, 1999).

The author wishes to thank the Anderson Center for Interdisciplinary Studies, the Leighton Studios at the Banff Center for the Arts, and the Blacklock Nature Sanctuary, where some of these poems were written, as well as the Jerome Foundation for two grants which allowed for the writing of the poems and the preparation of this manuscript.

First paperback edition, 2001

Tupelo Press
PO Box 539, Dorset, Vermont 05251
802.366.8185 • Fax 802.362.1883
editor@tupelopress.org • web www.tupelopress.org

Cover photograph: *Egg Florentine* by Susan Read Cronin, ©2000
Cover and book design by William Kuch, WK Graphic Design

For my Mother
Anne Sterle

Contents

I

Reflection ~3

Green ~ 4

Entering the Landscape ~ 6

Classification of the Tree World ~ 11

Nymphs ~ 12

II

Two Women

1 *Launched* ~ 17

2 *Connection* ~ 18

3 *Misunderstanding* ~ 19

4 *The Map* ~ 20

5 *Sparrow at My Window* ~ 21

6 *Reincarnations* ~ 22

7 *In the Desert* ~ 23

8 *Crossing Over* ~ 24

9 *Falling Into Place* ~ 25

10 *Question and Answer* ~ 26

11 *Tangle* ~ 27

12 *Another Voice* ~ 28

13 *Intruder* ~ 29

14 *From Memory* ~ 30

Octopus ~ 31

III

Snake ~ *35*

Making a Cross ~ *36*

The Hive ~ *37*

IV

Deciphering the Alphabet ~ *47*

Second Sight ~ *51*

After Visiting a Nature Conservancy Volunteer ~ *54*

A Single Gesture

1 *Cave Painting* ~ 55

2 *Church on the Hill* ~ 56

3 *Presence* ~ 57

4 *Dawn* ~ 58

5 *Animating Principle* ~ 59

6 *Abandoned Road* ~ 60

V

Habitat ~ 63

Triskelion ~ 64

Raven Watch ~ 66

Certain Moments Come ~ *71*

Notes ~ *79*

Four talked about the pine tree. One defined it by genus, species, and variety. One assessed its disadvantages for the lumber industry. One quoted poems about pine trees in many languages. One took root, stretched out branches, and rustled.

—Dan Pagis, *Conversation*, translated
from the Hebrew by Stephen Mitchell

If there is a mirror
the poet will always look into it . . .

—Tanikawa Shuntaro, *The Poet*

I

Reflection

The sky looks at itself in the water.
In the middle of an ordinary day,
a little whirlpool for the heart
when I drop a rock and clouds
break apart. It takes a certain
conception of the world to smash
the sun or wait to watch a crow
float from one shore to another.
It's the child in me. Pick up a stick.
Find a face hidden in the trees.
The naked girl is at it again.

Green

It starts with a tranquil thread,
a few more, then more and more.
A landscape is woven in:
nature's ubiquitous wick
announces itself in the invading grass,
grain-laden fields, in the commanding
canopy of a forest, the primal wash of the sea.
It demands attention in the edible,
vegetable world. It marries
every single flower. Hope claims it,
offering renewal, reproduction, youth.
Nothing can surpass it. It is impossible
to count its hues and shades and tints.
It is the color of vines and pines,
ferns and frogs, of stems and stalks.
It expresses love, justice,
the infancy of the world,
the light of the spirit. It blossoms
inside me, but there are days
relentless in their lack of promise
when the ambivalent fuse of joy
turns toward nausea, envy, ignorance.
It becomes a poisonous snake,
some slime, mold, pus, bad baloney.
It is a cancerous tumor, a maturing
bruise, disemboweled viscera.
Corrosive, it eats away at my life.
It is a paradox I cannot get my mind
around. In the midst of all this life
why so many thoughts of death?
I try to get back to that thread of inspiration.
What stops me? Like Nero, peering
through a polished emerald to watch

starving lions devour Christians,
I indulge it: the malignance,
the malaise, the mystery. I am gullible
to its charms. Stripped of everything
good in this world, I wait for a single
tendril to emerge, wait all day if I must
for the sedge and the spruce and the sage.

Entering the Landscape

1

A tree adapts to a position.
Dropped on a rock, the chance seed
steals nourishment where it can—
a lip of water, some flowerless moss.
Roots slender as spiders' legs
grip with a bold tenacious hold
the stone's uneven surface,
push down into a hairline crevice,
push deeper and deeper, not stopping
until they touch the transforming soil.

2

No more liberated seeds
or winged, crimson-tinted fruit.
What's planted grows.
The soil sends up its fixed idea,
shapes it into a shoot, a branch,
a bud. When a leaf appears
saw-toothed or bristle-tipped
or deeply fluted as a fish's fin,
it's easy to forget the time spent
packed in the bud, folded there
like a fan or rolled to fit
the tiny dome from which it rose.

3

The gods grow lean.
Disappearing a split second
before he reaches her,
Daphne metamorphoses
right there on the riverbank,

earth and water joining forces
so that the laurel will thrive,
so that Apollo, starved of love
by Cupid's wrathful arrow,
will have to watch as her feet
turn to roots that churn
into packed black earth, as bark
girds her girlish frame, rises
from toes to knees to stomach,
bark stretching up her fingers
to her wrists to her trembling arms,
bark spreading slowly across
her tender chest, her pale,
pale neck, bark inching higher
to obliterate her face, Apollo
dumbstruck by the weight of her
numb, petrified flesh, by the suddenly
cold heart, the rigid jaw, blocked ears,
by the unblinking eyes, the wooden
thighs, the newly unmoving lips.
The god's eyes widen as she
dips and bends, as her green skirt
sways, her mythic limbs rising
as a lover's might, but he turns away
when he tries to reach her cheek, touches
a blossoming pink twig, touches her leathery
leaves, those crooked, unyielding boughs.

4

What a torturous shape for a tree:
a straying crown, flimsy foliage,
the rugged homeliness of the bark,
a leggy trunk artless as a pencil,
the scant, unbalanced branches.
A large snapped bough dangles
downhill over an eroded bank.
Low sun lights the pendent branch

where hoarfrost has collected.
How clumsy it looks under its burden;
how cold against the snow-charged sky.
Its isolation attracts attention
the way a misshapen bush atop
a barren hilltop becomes a landmark.
No question where the eye will come to rest.
Though not as pleasing as the downy-coated
poplar, the polished holly, I've been given
this tree to plant in the soil of the page.

5

Let a tree be a tree.
Let its form intensify.
Bark of all barks.
Crown of crowns.
Let a tree be a tree
pushing toward the day's
simple light, turning
the way the wind turns,
turning as a flame
turns in the fire
when dried wood burns.

6

Illuminated by moonlight,
trees lose their detail.
From a distance,
even a well-trained eye
cannot see leaf scars
or scale-covered buds,
cannot determine the ratio
between short and long shoots,
cannot distinguish tree needles
flat as nail heads from four-
sided ones that exude a skunky

odor when they're crushed.
Only the shape is unique,
conforming to the habit of the tree.
Differences exist between
a steeple-shaped balsam fir
and a towering white spruce
even as blue panoramic shadows
fill the hollows between branches,
tier upon tier disappearing in the dusk.

7

In Delphi, the Pythian priestess
chewed leaves to induce oracular powers.
The moment the gods
poured their prophecies into her,
she must have cried out
as purely as a bird.
A note swelled inside her.
Birdsong spread through the boughs.
Music that's never stopped arriving.

8

In the expansive territory
between night and day,
sleep sways through dreaming trees,
through visionary evergreens,
ever-blooming, ever-bearing.
Breathing air scented by quilled pines,
we wake to find the parent bough
and its straying offshoots, an aging
elm log, ready for firewood,
breaking into blossom, the just
record of time and stress
seen in that gaunt skeleton
determined to defy
another century of storms.

Withdrawing into ourselves,
we take the world with us
and invent, all over again,
the circumference of our lives.

9

After an exquisite gray
washes over wintry trees
and familiarity fades,
dropping its leaves; after
shadows fall without distinction
and the road blurs into the bank,
the bank into the thicket; after
the cadence of falling snow,
the surrender that comes
with melting sunlight; after the resinous
sweetness of a forest, the habitual
wind, the theatrical landscape;
after the solitude, the harsh
solitude; after the inwardness,
the exile to the wooded slope;
after the vitality of the stalk,
the suave lines of a budding twig;
after the subtle undulations of a stem
and the graceful rhythm of a branch
and the dance, the dance
we must enter to understand,
my words crop the underwood
and sky breaks through tilting leaves
and the very quality of air is a poem.

Classification of the Tree World

" . . . the thing we apprehend in one great leap,
the thing that, by means of a fable, is
demonstrated as the exotic charm of another
system of thought, is the limitations of our own ..."
—Michel Foucault. *Les mots et les choses*

(1) Those Belonging to Birds;
(2) What may be Cut;
(3) Medicinal;
(4) Generated by Putrefaction;
(5) A Sequence of Shades at Dusk;
(6) Terrestrial;
(7) Found in Chalky Soil;
(8) Gaps in the Boughs;
(9) Drawn to Include an Effect of Snow;
(10) Fruit-Bearing;
(11) Indifferently Plentiful;
(12) The Harp of the Wind Plays Melodies;
(13) Leaves that Lie in One Plane;
(14) Et Cetera;
(15) Marked by the axman's eye; and
(16) That Allow Vigorous Wooing.

Nymphs

The first time
I went to the tree
was to knock on wood.

No one answered.
The second time I knocked,
the tree, wild in the wind,

leaned toward me.
No bad luck arrived.
I went back and knocked again

to tell the tree
my good fortune
was not forgotten.

•

Chiseling a nest hole
in dead wood,
a woodpecker drills a downed log.

The rapid blows of its beak
hammer me awake
each night for a week.

•

Beneath the bark
nymphs live
like hidden charms

people leave
in drawers or cupboards
for protection.

I believe in tree spirits
who embed their souls
in this wood.

•

They are not immortal

•

but their lives,
says Hesiod,
are ten times

that of the phoenix,
who outlives nine
ravens, who outlive

three glorious stags,
who outlive four
crows, who outlive

nine generations of aged men.

•

Beyond the shelter-
belts of farmsteads,
found deep

in poplar woods
and birch thickets,
a flicker assaults a tree

as nymphs
retreat into the tunneled
ruts of the trunk.

The bird chips away
without distraction.
Its showy

red patch,
a splash of blood,
catches my eye.

•

Tender

wing buds
of an immature insect

are like the rising
nipples of a
young girl.

The temptation
to slide a finger
over the small mounds . . .

•

Fly away!

•

The nymphs are free,
changed forever
as they brush

the pond's scalloped edge.
What part of me they take away
will settle some day

deep in dying wood.
I will be there
when you knock.

II

Two Women

1 *Launched*

You spun complicated webs across the page.
Across every page. From every corner
of every page. Intricate strands.
Stringy black veils of ink. You drew them
compulsively, out of boredom, in every class.
Each thread cast out to catch
the startled heart. How I squirmed
seeing spiders flee down a drain or
into drafty cracks of a wall. Soon,
webs were everywhere: spread out in corners
and window casings, settled in petals of a flower,
angled on fences, among rocks, between
leaves of low trees, the loose lacework
sagging in the slightest breeze, and there you were
head down in the middle, puzzling each passerby
with the extravagant riddle of your legs.

2 *Connection*

Thousands of silken webs
fanned the swamp at dawn,
hung from broken limbs of scrub pine,
tipped back fronds of densely clustered
parsley fern, floated ghostly
above ground fog, spreading delicate
white veils leaf to leaf to leaf,
the diaphanous nets tucked
into every corner of that swamp,
connecting seedstalk to tree stump,
connecting with finely spun filament
the dewy foliage far as the eye
could see. I stepped forward
carefully, shyly, my whole heart
caught by the immaculate strands,
the intricate geometry visible
one brief hour before morning sun
destroyed any trace of its existence.
What I saw was what the world
concealed, what surfaced
for a moment and was gone.

3 *Misunderstanding*

Why didn't I understand
when I left that drunken party to follow you
down a pathless crust of snow
spreading through the meadow; why,
after weeks of awkwardness between us,
didn't I understand when you reached out
to the scar's faint stitch on my finger, touched
the loosened hair windblown at my back?
How could I have misunderstood
when you recited the moments we'd shared
or dared to speak of the loneliness
you'd dragged into that cold March day?
Couldn't you see I was skittish as the bird
my mother had crafted for me
as a Christmas present—the mutilated wing,
the harsh string she'd used on its heart?

4 *The Map*

Lost. Your map scissored by roads
I couldn't find as the sun's shoulder
pressed at my back.
Not a single whitewashed house
anywhere in sight. I cursed
whatever I saw—the half-eaten
carcass sprawled in a ditch,
wilting crops, delinquent crows.
And tell me, where did that long-legged
sunflower come from with its lopsided head?

A noisy bee blew past my face,
followed a trace of fragrance
a half-mile or more. Already I knew,
as I walked toward those two cows
sculptured in the distance, I'd make a wrong turn.
The wind would mislead me.
Somewhere between A and B
a new path would emerge
then retreat, would divide in half,
and the map would be an open hand,
revealing all the roads I could have taken.

5 *Sparrow at My Window*

Atop an open shutter, nesting
in a mass of matted feathers,
dried grass, it sang
nonstop, a shrill,
high-pitched chirping.
A sparrow woke my sleeping life:
teck teck   teck teck   teck teck.
Ready to fly off as a rising sun
lit the sky like a lantern,
ready to fly off
after crickets and crabgrass seeds,
it was overexcited, the quick,
monotonous cries repeating
teck teck   teck teck   teck teck.
But when I considered the heart
was twenty percent of its total weight,
no wonder the song didn't stop.
How it must have leapt awake,
so much struggling to assert itself
above the freshturned garden.

6 *Reincarnations*

Because one day I will send my soul
into another's body, I went back
to the microbe, smaller than a speck
of dust, back to the bug-eyed fly,
the greedy bee, the scaly toad,
back to the black-feathered bird
roosting on a barn roof,
staring at a scorched field,
a plow's idle blade. How easily
I went back to the tent caterpillar
wrapping monotonous wheels around
sprouting tines of scouring rush.
But there were others,
born of darkness or divine
displeasure, nailed to the mind's
whitewashed walls. When was it
I put them there, adding a winged boar,
a goat-headed horse? If I hadn't believed
I could live through anything
and survive, I wouldn't have dared;
I wouldn't have dared reach out to one
who navigates a weightless gulf of air.

7 *In the Desert*

It took us an hour to find an Apache plume,
a six-foot shrub, flowering,
silvery puffs of fruit heads borne
at the tips of interwoven branches,
and from the rim of a small cup, five white petals
flower after flower after flower.
On that gritty slope where an ash-throated
flycatcher sang high in a Joshua-tree,
I didn't know how to respond to its
low, rolling *queee-eer, queee-eer,* lost as I was
without those familiar northern lakes,
their wide-open bellies of water. I didn't know
what to say to your words of *love* and *forever*
that shifted in me uneasily as sand burning
underfoot. No, I didn't know how to turn into
somebody else, into someone who could love
your naked smile, your beautiful hands.

8 *Crossing Over*

Up a rocky path rising from the riverbank,
I climbed, a whistle of steam in my chest,
face red and shiny as skin under a scab.
A hundred yards ahead, perched
on a branch of a rotted black ash,
a double-crested cormorant preened in the air,
its orange throat pouch barely visible
as the neck stretched to tail feathers
fanned out like a deck of cards.
In an impulse of pure release,
it flared its wings to absorb the last
pleats of light through summer trees.
Another cormorant grunted from the water,
puffed out its feathery crown in a shake,
swam downstream, the hooked bill
tilted as it followed the sedge
framing the edge of the river, shifting
its attention from water to woods,
from woods back to water. I walked
slowly through this scene, unnoticed
as if my steps were nothing more
than indifferent flickers of wind.
Stopping in my own shadow, I crossed over,
the moment lifting me forward in flight.

9 *Falling Into Place*

Meeting in morning fog
    that clouded the riverbank,
        we turned to kiss,

an unguarded moment
    when a body loses
        its boundaries with the world.

However did it happen?
    There were so many
        familiar places

to hide,
    so little tenderness
        present in my life.

How could I have
    dared abandon
        what I'd known

and given myself to you,
    blind as an egg
        in a trout's

leaping belly—
    but I believed
        the splash I heard

was blessing,
    trusted
        its quick measure

of possibility,
    felt it rise up in me,
        and I followed.

10 *Question and Answer*

Over the plush ruffles
where the moon had fallen,

wind, stuttering across water,
asked, *How will it come out?*

Gusting up, it blurred
a stand of spindly birch.

Undecided it withdrew,
leaning back

settled but distant.
Another damp flow of air

pushed up from the lake.
What will become of you?

From question to answer
it was one glance

at loosely swaying trees,
and I saw how my thoughts

had always followed
those reckless currents

surging
over open water,

the ones that kick up
beyond a break in the road

then rush headlong
into oncoming traffic.

11 *Tangle*

You came to me as light,
the first threads of the day
shining through an open window,
crossing the warped floorboards
to my bed, weaving itself
into every gesture you made.
How could I turn away?
And yet, after a morning of love,
after months of mornings, after habit
had tangled me up inside,
I began to dream about a spider
whose web wasn't seen
unless I was moving into light.
It would hang for hours
upside down, waiting
at the edge of consciousness,
waiting for me to step toward it,
and in a moment still as a first kiss,
the thrill of what was to come
quivered up my spine, and I'd
lose myself in my own reflection.

12 *Another Voice*

Wherever we went
I searched for something else,
expecting it to fly out when I found
two mottled eggs in a bowl of grass,
expecting to feel more than wheat
brush my cheek when the field parted.
Was it because of this
that thistles bared their teeth
or that my tongue touched
the white thread of a worm
needling the apple's heart?
Wherever we went
it left a trace of itself
like the powdery wings of a moth.
Whatever it was, called and called
and kept on calling, its faraway voice
beckoning me to come away.

13 *Intruder*

Mid-December,
twenty-seven degrees below zero,
but they were out there:
five scavengers in a ditch
circling another who'd turned
downwind to land, head feathers tousled,
wings ragged as weathered flags.
What a shock to watch
all five screech forward,
beaks aimed at the intruder.
That's all I saw.
All I wanted to see.
I drove on, my own errands
moving me town to town,
my own trespass too painful
to face whatever happened next.
By the time I returned to that spot
five hours later, all of them were gone,
the only sign a clawed dish
of old snow and one fallen feather,
its black arrow pointing north
toward a deeper white
which is where I decided to go.

14 *From Memory*

Years from now
I might invent a different day,
new regrets. I might forget
boats harbored in the bay,
the dull-gray mist, or gulls
screeching out of sight,
forget how a drab breeze
blew through the leather-leaf,
how I tried not to lose myself
in the mutable weather of your eyes.
Sitting atop a rocky outcrop,
you talked about a future
I could no longer picture
together. Better to forget
all the unuttered words
shadowy as fish in the water
and the loud, deaf waves
crashing at our feet.
Nobody saw us there.
There was nobody out there
to say *you frowned;*
she stood up. Nobody
to see you walk away, to see me
dampen with surf spray as I watched
an uncleated skiff slip out to sea.

Octopus

Beyond
    the sandy beach,
        the coral shore,

beneath a steep
    ledge of rock,
        down

where the heavens have drowned,
    down
        to the dark ocean floor,

an undulating wave begins,
    a whirlwind
        under water.

Like the vortex
    made by a sinking ship,
        long furls

unfold
    and swirl,
        luring bright-

striped fish
    to the ruffling
        seaweed of its arms.

How it changes
    red to black
        in one convulsive flash

with its elastic sac,
    its radiating ring
        of muscles.

Those wormy tentacles
    circling an overgrown
        head can be

deceiving—
    the hypnotic sway,
        the nonthreatening stir

of the cerebral
    and then, without
        forewarning,

it recoils,
    expels
        a cloud of ink

to stun the senses.
    O cunning,
        skillful,

patient stalker,
    O Athena of the deep,
        you offer

the Gorgon's face,
    eight snaking locks
        stream down

like rays of light
    around
        a chartless center.

III

Snake

Saw it hatch from an egg
like a bird, saw it surge
months later from a mud hole,
glide across a log, wave upon wave,
into a dark crevice in the rocks,
saw its feathery tongue flicker
as its eyes went cold,
and it swelled thick-bodied
until it burst from its skin
in one luminous stroke, saw
the undulating string of chevrons
shiver down its back,
saw it slip into the world
in roots and umbilical cords,
wheels and smoke and curling hair,
saw it in the whip-tailed wind
hissing behind me, in the uterine earth,
the Great Serpent writhing under my feet
when I walked. Saw it coil
into a wreath, and still it stirred
without arms or legs or wings, slithered forward,
unlocked its jaw over a mouse, unlocked
something in me: Lord of this world,
Lord who delights in blood,
and my shovel crushed its head,
and this is how I yielded.

Making a Cross

Of 385 varieties, to make the simplest
all you need are two sticks:
one vertical; the other, horizontal.
Call one time; one, space or
life—death, good—evil, male—female.
You choose. Any polarity will do
as long as the cross-piece cuts across
the one upright. Now, it's a human form
with arms outstretched. Rub them together.
A couple of sparks, a few more,
a flash of light, a slow increase in heat,
and radiating around you: uncontainable fire.

The Hive

1

In winter, I tunnel through snow.
In spring, it's the plow.
A thousand cuts in the field.
In summer, a thorn
scrapes a bloody furrow in my skin.
Ditches fill with color.
Trees, once green, go bare to the top.
My feet make a trench in the leaves
as an insistent bee
rises from the underbrush.
Does it expect to soothe me
when it kisses my hand?

2

I wanted you
as much as you ever
wanted me, but
I waited
while the first gray hairs
appeared on my head,
waited for the stars'
glacial drift around a snowy comet
that comes once a century,
its fading tail
luminous as fishline,
waited for the other woman
to die or divorce,
waited long after I refused.
I was left waiting
while bees hummed in their hives
and winter choked
the river's throat with ice.

3

Amid green thumbs of weeds,
a most common flower
sends up from masses of dark,
deeply-cut leaves, tall blue blossoms.
Just opened, it lures a visiting bee
that zigzags flower to flower,
disappears inside a petal's puckered skirt.
Eurydice, I think. When I turn, a head
powdered with white pollen emerges,
and the shadow mine makes
moves plant by plant around the garden.

4

The day I found
the plump corpse of a bee
lying motionless on the window sill,
I held it in my hand.
Cradling its velvet-coated body,
I noticed my own lifeline
like an arrow underneath it,
while outside, toiling bees
crisscrossed in the sun.
Consider the bee and see how she labours.

5

Everywhere in the exotic
flowering of that garden, bees
soared and hovered, wings
beating the air, heart-shaped heads
visible on honeysuckle and catkins
collecting acres of pollen, the world
astir around me. It was there,
between the dense notes of your pulse,
you kissed me, bewildered

about where to place this moment
given our complicated lives.
Days later the tremor you sent through me
returned: the aftershock of bees
drawing nectar to make
a single drop of honey.

6

Look at the beehive you've made of my heart
Look at the swarm clustering around me
and the wax I use
trying to seal myself off
Look at what you've become
a bear
clumsy and mulish
Look at yourself
nosing the feathery ferns
the milky-colored mushrooms
ignoring the dizzy funnel of bees at your back
Look at the muscles bunch in your legs
then stretch the long length of a tree
Look at your claws thrusting toward me
your muzzle smeared
by the dripping honey
Look at me tremble
Look at the paper-thin comb
wedged between my ribs
Look at it
then tell me again how the wind you miss
sleeps in my hair
again
about the tangled hues in my eyes.

7

Inhabited by bees.
Spring still burning in my eyes.
The intricate dance
home from the flower.
In my deepest thoughts,
the smell of the hive.

I surrender to it all.

My heart is thick with pleasure,
but I'll tell you
about the holes inside,
the honeycomb
I've worked for years to fill.

8

A secluded nest
and bees
breathing beneath my ribs.
A scent of clover in the air.

Certain summer nights
love comes to me
frantic for meaning.
I haven't got the answer,

but I know how honey
sweetens the tongue,
how my own blood hums
from the bee's nimble bite.

9

First the swarm tone,
then a dense cloud forming,
the impetuous flight

to limb or random stump,
fence or ladder where bees
alight. Are these the ones
Aristaeus saw sicken and die,
that touched the lips of Pindar
and Plato lying helplessly
in their cradles, that crossed
the lips of St. Ambrose
before entering his mouth?

10

The greedy bee returns to its hive
with sticky feet, a packed pollen basket.
Half-drunk from venturing
beyond the petal's crease
and into the trumpet-throated lily
drooping on the garden wall,
it drones, the same sound
that flows through my veins
as we sleep, side by side
across a continent, our words
holding us together like the thin
cells of a hive. Is this the unhesitating life
I was meant to lead?
Many chambers? Much noise?

11

From my pursed mouth,
a single word
works its way out
like a pillow feather
then floats to the floor,

but I'm not ready for the truth,
cannot ask who or when or why.
Why bother with explanations

when my tongue is dead in my mouth,
and thoughts half-crazed in my head.

I stare out at a frozen landscape,
at moonlit gardens of ice
spreading over the fields,
at a fraction of light, so far off,
shining at me from the other side.

12

A hum of bees from dry lips
all night in my ear:
a swarm of words inside a crimson flower.

It clings to me—the sugary
smear of honey on my hands,
pollen dusting my breast.

What frightens me awake,
lighting a flame deep in my cheek?

I fly out of myself,
all that we love between us.

13

From an open window,
a breeze blows in
thin bandages of fog.

The black night softens.
On the fringe of audibility,
the truth draws near.

14

The moment they'd sensed
thick puffs of smoke

filling the hive
the feral bees forgot
their tending and readied
themselves to abandon it.

Gorged on honey, too full
to bend into stinging position
for defense, the docile workers
forgot how singlemindedly
they'd returned from those snow asters
spreading through the meadow.

Spooked by fire
from a smoldering bee smoker
that smelled of pine needles
and sumac bobs, they ate their way
into a stupor while the beekeeper
cut that dead limb and carried it away.

15

When your letter appeared,
I held it for an hour, remembering
the way our bodies joined
one last time to say good-bye.
I barely spoke for a month,
my words falling away
as I stared at snow swirling
a thousand miles between us.
Not even a warm day
could woo me into the world
to watch the bees' brief
thistledown flight.
You never wrote again, but
I will tell you about memory,
the crust it formed so I could heal,
the scab I picked until it bled.

16

For months winter disguised
the hidden hive body
nobody touched, but after spring
melted the last snow from my hand
and all that was unsaid
vanished in a river of water,
the slow-headed bees
dropped from the comb
one by one, half-starved,
the colony so strong
they'd run out of food
weeks before any flowers would bloom.
I put out pots of sugared syrup
to save them. It was only a matter of time.
How could I stop those clumsy,
richly-veined wings from stirring inside?

17

How sharply the thorn stuck in my finger,
how reliable my blood
making its own rose in my hand,

and this memory of you:

a petal
the flower didn't feel
when it fell . . .

IV

Deciphering the Alphabet

Winter advances
leaving its white tracks
bounding over the hills
I climb each December
to get to the river
where velvety shrews,
voles and squirrels
crisscross in the snow,
their claw marks
reminding me of the exquisitely
complicated pattern
I watched an Ojibwe
bite into birchbark.
(*Art as old as the world,*
the woman said to me.)

•

In the origin myth of Eskimos
the first children
sprouted from fertile soil
and, like tender plants,
stayed rooted there,
being nourished by the earth.
No one knows how one boy
and one girl grew into adults
able to walk into the world,
able to meet and marry.

•

Each tree
was a letter once.
Pagans
spelled out their secrets
by threading

the proper leaves
in proper order—
Birch tree, Heather leaf,
leaf of the Ash.
A language
you could hold in your hand.
Words that quivered,
turned color in the fall,
that could be taken back,
burned in regret.
Lonely winters
when there was nothing
to say.

•

From a north window,
the choked river,
a slippery crack of light.
Does my neighbor notice me
crouched down,
my bare fingers exploring
the deer tracks I've found,
some chips in the ice?
I wave once,
but she stares
absentmindedly into the cold.
Pure imitation.
The great bored glacier of her face.

•

How many have known
the endless emptiness
inside an ordered room?
How many, a silence
so profound, inside
and out?

•

I turn, startled,
as if someone
dogged my steps.
Nothing.
Midday sun
scatters down
among sapling ash.
At my feet, birdtracks
wherever I look.
The only ciphers of the day.
My footprints merge
with the ones laid down here,
my whole body,
heart, lung, muscle,
leaving its trace.

•

Everything that moves
leaves a story. No story
can exist by itself.

•

What am I
to the wolf and the rabbit and the fox?
To the songless birds
balancing on branches?
To the solitary pines
dipped in frost?

•

First the trough
where it plowed forward,
then the wide belly-slide
down the bank,
the musty scent-post,

the scat, the smooth hole
where the otter slipped
through a window in the ice.
Scattered all around,
a wolverine's fresh tracks,
the slashes where its claws
raked as it slid to a stop.
Stiff gusts of wind
kick up around me.
Twigs and bits of debris
soon mar the tracks.
Before long, the sharp edges
will begin to slump.
By early next week,
everything will be erased,
the immaculate snow
unable to keep the shape
of a single creature.

Second Sight

1

Found stunned northside of Townline Road,
the snowy owl drove boxed in my car
two hours to reach the raptor volunteer
who held the half-blind bird overnight
then rode four more hours before
delivering it, disoriented,
to a steel table where men
took a sharpened scalpel to its head.

2

In my cupped hand, the real
fruit of Eden: smooth, leathery,
thick-skinned, forbidden for its
crimson juice, thin vesicles,
dripping pulp. The venous-
colored seed Persephone welcomed
into her mouth. It was the owl
perched at the threshold of Hell
who saw her swallow, who
denounced her for obediently
swallowing. It was the owl.

3

A deep sweetness on the tongue.
The simple *yes* I give
to the things I love.

4

Thrashing in the closed
coffin of that box, the owl punched
holes in old cardboard where

the hooked beak broke through.
Specks of blood and battered feathers
littered the makeshift nest.
No matter the effort,
wings failed to bring it to flight.

5

Over the pitched spine of an abandoned barn,
a ghostly owl, over snow rows
and fence posts, over chips of bottle glass
flashing in a ditch and the deserted,
undiminished miles, over the emotional
weight of that road, it crosses
straight out in front of me,
and the car so accurate as it skids
on ice, slides trunk-first into a tree.

6

Where the moon has been shining,
a predatory eye
and something breathing
beyond the gate where the cemetery lies.

7

Like pond lilies floating open,
unspoiled feathers
drape my gloved hand,
but I feel claws leafing out,
gripping me, not wanting to let go.
Behold the convulsive dive,
the heartstopping drop as it breaks
a crust of snow to take exactly what it wants.

8

A savage, unlucky creature,
the Chinese say, terrifying
because it devours the mother.
Yet how do you judge one
that eats what it sees,
sees what it eats?

9

The moon: no light of its own—
it is all reflection.

10

Those milky wings hunt me
into the night as if I were harmless
as a field mouse or tree frog
offering nothing
but a penny of consciousness
as it dies. My eyes close.
I whirl down,
a tide of bones at my feet.

11

One eye changes places with another.
The owl swivels its neck,
sees me with one good eye. A moon appears,
and I float there, my reflection
gliding in icy light. There I am
fully seen for the first time.
There I am, fingers brushing its neck—
out of foolishness or arrogance
or grace—stroking it as I would
a lover's brow, touching my lips
to the dangerous pillow of its head.

After Visiting
a Nature Conservancy Volunteer

Driving north through Wisconsin, past Lulu Lake,
the Muckwonago River, I recited her list of pests:
bindweed, burdock, leafy sponge,
pondweed, milfoil, plumeless thistle,
identified the scenery as I went—fen, sedge meadow,
bog, shrub-carr—stopped to watch cricket frogs
and Cooper's hawks, filled the lakes with bluegill,
spotted bass, long-eared sunfish, star-headed
minnows, filled the woods with hickory and hackberry,
paper birch, let my tongue roll over tussock bulrush,
northern kittentail, Blandings' turtles, thought about
how language cries out for a subject, how self
and subject merge in the black-bibbed sparrow,
the honeybee wooed from a brimming hive,
the triumphant pokeweed tasseled in white.

A Single Gesture

1 *Cave Painting*

Sealed by fallen debris, the cave
closed into absolute darkness

leaving undiscovered a prehistoric,
wooly-haired rhino that roamed the walls

while overhead a great-horned owl soared
unseen for a hundred-thousand years,

claws opening over a rat-like smudge
crouched in the corner, and a lone hunter,

a blackened stick figure without hair or flesh
or organs, shot arrows at a beast

asleep near a dirty pool of water. This
is what the finders found as they dug

through layers of mud and matted leaves,
broke through the grim lair of history

as a blinding sun began to translate
pictures they couldn't even see at first,

complicated, as the past always is,
by the uncolored light within.

2 *Church on the Hill*

It looks down on the city
growing back from the riverbank.

It is full of people and the people
full of prayers that should rise to heaven

but spiral to the sprawling water,
turn brown along the edges

like so many apple-skins
peeled from the fruit of trees

kneeling by that river. All
rots with time, even hope

with its bruised hue
spreading across the grove below.

3 *Presence*

As I cross the north field,
first it's the bleached teeth

then a bald patch of grass—
nothing left but a beak and feathers—

then a spray of porcupine quills
sticking from a bloated body

then a stag with both eyes
rolled back into its head

as if in trance,
lying in the greening pasture,

listening to long harp-strings of wire
whine in the unseen air.

In the insistent presence of the dead,
crows rush down like arrows.

4 *Dawn*

A peerage of birds
perches in

sweet-smelling cedar.
How small they seem

resting lightly
on leafless branches.

When a church bell's
metal tongue

counts the hour,
they twirl up

white-winged
into the expansive air,

rise in a weightless stream,
waken the day inside me.

The hour vanishes with the birds,
and in that vanishing,

another world
behind the low-changing clouds

sends down its bridge of light.
My heart opens

faithfully as Blake's at Peckham Rye
when angels filled the tree.

5 *Animating Principle*

So we will never be alone
they come

becoming
bog pine or raked leaves

or a chain of lakes, becoming
fog folded into

the tangled arms of birch,
becoming fresh plums

and squatting dogs, chicory
and ragwort, becoming a putrid

patch of swamp or struggling
cornrows or a cat's tail

spongy with mud. So we will
never be alone they become

ants and squirrels and ravens,
snowstorms and tangerines.

Multiplying around us,
they fill the deeper world

into which spirit may enter
so we will never be alone.

6 *Abandoned Road*

Stalled in iron-colored mud,
a rusted truck. The woman's walked

back to the farmhouse for the night
having sworn at the grinding engine for an hour.

A trio of crows has given up
its flagrant squawking. Even

the deer have departed to bed down
deeper in the woods, leaving behind

a path of trampled grass. The moon's
tapering light shines off the chrome.

There is only moon and chrome and mud
and newly budded twigs hanging off

five hundred acres of trees. This is the world
philosophers say disappears when it isn't seen,

an unteachable region of the mind, begging
faith, and for those who fall in love with it,

faith begins with a single gesture
inward and ends outside in grace.

V

Habitat

It is the hollow where the landscape
dips to a frost pocket. It is the evening's
heavy air rolling from the uplands.
It is the trapped breath that kills
all but the most tolerant grasses.
How cruel spring can be.

Out of nowhere, ten-thousand lives.
The marsh is awash with their courtship calls.
The marsh is teeming, but that swampy water
scarcely moves. Atop a muskrat's haystack house,
a pair of red-winged blackbirds. Perched on bur reeds
and bulrushes and cattail clumps, a hundred more.

What a dense congregation: turtles and rabbits,
ducks, toads, coots, rails, wrens, untold insects
dabbling at mire's edge, as well as jewelweed,
arrowhead, sweetflag, sedge. Somehow it survives:
the seeds and nests and floating algal mats,
the soft-stemmed pondweeds, the feathery debris.

Somebody wants all this to exist.
Somebody wants me in the midst of this existence.
I no longer ask who or why but turn the way the world
turns and put my faith in the quick-tongued
cricket frog who, drawn to the safety of this basin,
aims as it lifts up, squeezes both eyes shut—and leaps.

Triskelion

Stabia quocunque ieceris:
It will stand erect wherever it is thrown.

Three legs
radiate
like a swift-

moving insect's
in harmony around
a fixed center.

In it you see
the sun's
first rising,

the zenith
high in
noontime sky,

then the inevitable
slide
as it settles

at horizon's edge,
a rotating
swastika of light:

creation,
preservation,
ruination,

the cosmic
whirlpool
always in motion.

Triple-footed legs
bend at the knee,
join at the thigh,

a single
pelvic arch
between them.

I tell you,
there *is*
a divine center of being,

a primal thought
from which
we sprang . . .

Raven Watch

God feeds the ravens.
—Sylvia Plath, *Letters Home*

1

A bulky mass of sticks,
the cup lined
with moss and fur
and dry gray lichens.
Seven dull green eggs.
Seven songbirds.
Seven magicians.

2

How many voices
in one voice?
A hollow, wooden *wonk*,
a guttural croaking,
a low-pitched
tolling bell, a hoarse
cur-ruk, cur-ruk,
a deep-toned *croo*,
croo, croo, a chattering tongue
with its dangerous news,
its panic.

3

Noah commanded a raven
to seek land, watched it
fly off alone
over the water's overflowing womb.
It did not return.
Noah cursed it: *wanderer*,
restless, unclean.

4

Carrion-feeder.
It could live anywhere
but neglects its young
until bristly tufts hide
the newborn nostrils, until
lance-shaped feathers
blacken the squawking throats.
Speak to me of providence:
He giveth food to the young
ravens that cry.

5

Blood, the raven's drink.
Its unappeasable hunger
sudden and black
in an icy ditch.
When feeding, first
it eats the eyes, pulls out
the eyes of covetousness and sin.
Blood bird. Blood bird.
Confession and penance
are the raven's.

6

Messenger of death.
Protector of prophets.
Trickster. Shape-shifter.
Befriender of witches.
Shy one. Wary one.
Solitary sorcerer.
On the Tree of Knowledge
from which Eve
gathers the fruit, it sits.

7

What does it foretell?
The starving mind decides.

8

Seeker of answers.
From the thorn hedge
it watches the woods,
threshold without mercy,
watches but does not speak.
Dual-natured talking bird,
the tongue's split tip
knows how to prize out
what it wants.

9

I can't help myself.
Riding a rising current,
it soars, crying above me,
a raven with a Roman nose,
a hole torn through
its wing's metallic cloak.
I can't help myself.
My own misshapen call
returns to me. Back
and forth, the two of us
call back and forth.
Curious, it circles,
tumbles once, a swift
flip, luring me
into its high-flying arc.

10

Straight through the hole
and into the void like a button
into the vast darkness
which is home
to all that is not yet
in form, it leads me,
pecking at the door, pecking
beyond fear, pecking like the ravens
on Odin's shoulders, one
called *thought*, one, *memory*.

11

Eventually,
everything flies inward
toward the source, roils together
so you cannot see
anything anymore, not
a single familiar shape.
You will never be the same.
No car or cow track
will get you there,
but you'll always meet a raven
towering between two worlds.

12

A raven screams.
How many years have flown by?
The yard is bright with snow.
The woven nest is empty.

13

Taking the dead to the sky,
the bird's wide oars
row across blue water,
row tirelessly across
familiar ground.

14

Something ancient
peers from the pit
of its eye. I do not fear it.
Cras, cras,
cras, cras, cras.
On its Latinate tongue,
the word *tomorrow.*

Certain Moments Come

1

The sludge-colored truck,
speeding toward its next delivery,
braked with a blind
mechanical strength, skidded
fifty feet, rammed my car
broadside, didn't stop—
the rutted gravel road
slid past and rust-red leaves
lashed across the windshield
and wind made dust
to cover up what happened.
Blood gurgled up my throat
while the suddenly tilting world
touched my forehead
with its dizzy thoughts.
I was so alone, so startled by it.
What's dead and dying
fills the autumn air.
I smell it wherever I go.

2

On the October tree:
three shriveled leaves, drab
brown and barely hanging on.
An idle gust of wind blows them
into the hurt world whose piles
dry at my feet. Bundled children—
ah, the plump wings of their arms—
play among damaged limbs, cut
branches, wind-bent weeds. Everything

will feed the fire. It's as if winter
steals the leaves, and a skeleton,
a skeleton stands for your life.

3

Dead light from a star far away
shines off fields of frosted stubble
picked clean by hungry crows.
Cold and lost in thought, I follow
a loosened string of fencewire,

my aching lungs a honeycomb of ice.
Spotting a discarded feather, I bring its velvet
delicacy to my cheek. One simple gesture
unlocks the heart. Blackbird, blackbird,
your discomforting cries come alive in my mouth.

4

Three inches of new snow
and a full moon in the garden

and the dozens of ways
we've learned to say *I love you*.

It was a kind of aphrodisiac—
the world opening again to possibility—

but this time, the words we spoke
were *cancer* and *surgery*,

and in that exaggerated moment,
we reached out as if for the last time,

already knowing what the world
would come to mean without the other,

but I was not prepared for your blood everywhere—
between our legs, on our bellies, streaked

across the sheets. Sharp cries filled the room
as we rushed to wash ourselves clean,

not yet ready for the final question
we ask about our lives, not yet ready . . .

as water bled red down the drain's cold throat.

5

Dumped back into darkness.
Everyone gets a turn. It happens
even to saints this temptation
to despair. It might begin with a few
discontented branches rising then falling
with the saddest of gestures. It might
start one snowy day when the world
goes deaf to your voice. You sigh
but no one hears. The sky is gray.
The river creeps by with its mushy ice.
Sometimes a dream will get you there
when the one you love appears pale
and statue-still in a gravedigger's cart.
The future yellows like old corn
left too long on the stalk. Ask those
happier than you; they'll tell you
nothing lasts forever. Start with saplings,
and before you know it, scavengers arrive.

6

Were it not for the delight of feeding,
carcasses would litter the ground
so thank the fox, wolf, and raven
that attack the dead with their hunger,

the swarming bottleblue flies and grubs,
minuscule gnats that lay black eggs
in putrid water, even hard-winged beetles
extracting glutinous matter out of dung
cattle drop in the field until it's
light as the dust wind carries
miles before it slows. No bones
to be dragged to an open hole
then mournfully shoveled closed.
Each fallen tree rots and crumbles
offering itself to fungi and slime mold,
spiders, bark lice, earwigs. What a simple end
for all things short-lived, fast-growing,
so why do I squirm imagining worms
wrapped around an eye socket
or sticking like bandages to your
discolored, decomposing bones?

7

The air is dense with birds
as if something could happen,
as if a wing could be torn,

as if memory,
most fragile of all wings,
could hold forever what is torn.

This thinning wind
barely keeps my
far-flying thoughts afloat.

The one I love flies through this poem.
Now, every bird is one bird,
every branch conquered by its weight.

8

The snow goose's neck:
a slender stem
where winter grows.
It leads me
straight to field-hardened wheat
stretching all the way to the horizon.
A part of me goes with it.
All birds should be as white
as it is, the whole world
as it is: wing after wing,
each thought cold
and clean, feathered
and flying.

9

Mid-winter,
the landscape dreary
and utterly remote,
I'm aware of your face,
the cast of ashes
I see in your face:
that same slate color
first perceived by a newborn
whose world stays
bathed in gray, whose eyes
accept color gradually
over the next few years.
Here we are, together,
back at the beginning again.
Here we are, dismayed
by that leaden sky,
these circular days.

10

No angels this year,
just a wing of snow the wind
tossed on the porch.
It wasn't like a bird.
Not at all heavenly.
It came with the force of
wilderness behind it
when it swept over me,
blurred my vision.
There was no rejoicing, but
it found the shape of my face
just before it fell.

11

A peak of snow on the cut trunk:
a little requiem of white
covering growth rings
nested inside each other
so closely in this northern clime
they are impossible to count.
On my own finger, a ring.
Let me recite the vows.
Night after night.
Like a slish of oil across the skin.
I'm happy now, I'm happy.
Don't die. Don't ever go away.

12

In the lightning—
        oh, but the sky,
too, was part of it,
        its gloomy mood
sinking into
        narrow-needled pines

and then that repetitive
        boom   boom   boom
until a tree trunk exploded in one
        magnificent pop, cracked
in half, its defeated crown
        head-down outside
the hospital window.
        If prayer means
launching out of the heart
        towards God,
then surely I prayed
        each time another bolt
sent down its strict
        tightrope of light.

13

Ditchwater eases off the sandbags'
swollen hip, a provisional pause
on its way downhill to the churchyard
basement where run-off leaks
between cement cracks, oozes
around worn brickwork, seeps into
the carpet where children sit
on folding chairs, their own hands
folded in prayer. For a time,
it loses itself before emerging
beyond mossy gravestones
and straightaway from the afterlife
promised here, from the black-backed
Bible, the faithful with scripture trained
to habit on their tongues, committed
to its own course, its own muddy path,
gathering speed as it goes until it sounds
stunned by its own daring, and birds
waken in the swallowed fields
where everything freed and floating is
unleashed at last from the straitjacket of winter.

14

Today it is coltsfoot with petaled suns
overrunning the roadside, drowsy flowers
bowing to that red thread in the east
I follow as if it were Ariadne's light.
Last week, two thousand miles away,
it was a jellyfish with its single satin lung
fluttering in water. And before that,
a wafer of ice in a pocked metal saucepan
I left by the garden. Months ago,
after the hospital and the tubes and the blood,
it was the way that new scar slept
on my husband's body, how the gold
wedding ring, worn smooth as a relic, felt
between my fingers as I rubbed his hand.
It could be almost anything. Certain moments come
when I turn away from the heart-shaking darkness
that governs a life, away from the odylic crows,
the decay I'm forever stirring into soil.

Notes

Entering the Landscape is for Fran Blacklock. In Section 9, lines 21 and 22 are an allusion to a quotation from St. John at Ephesus: "If you have not entered the dance, you mistake the event."

Two Women: The Koran 29:40 was the inspiration for this poem: *But verily, the frailest of all houses surely is the house of the spider.*

The Hive: Consider the bee and see how she labors is from Proverbs.

After Visiting a Nature Conservancy Volunteer is for Shirley Ellis.

Triskelion: There are triskelions formed from three human legs bent at the knee. Armored legs in this configuration appear in the arms of the Isle of Man with this motto: *Stabia quocunque ieceris.*

Raven Watch: He giveth food to the young ravens that cry is from Psalms.

Certain Moments Come: Section 14, line 4 is an echo from Göran Sonnevi's poem *The narrow shaft*, translated by Rika Lesser.